Little Lizard

AT HOME IN THE RAIN FOREST

WRITTEN BY JENNIFER BOUDART
ILLUSTRATED BY GARY TORRISI

Publications International, Ltd.

A baby lizard climbs out of her egg, buried beneath the sands of the tropical rain forest. Little Lizard is a green iguana lizard, but her sharp claws and the scales along her back make her look a lot like a tiny dragon.

In the rain forest, the sunlight filters through the leafy treetops and bounces off her green skin. She shines like a jewel.

Other lizards crawl around in the sand. They're Little Lizard's brothers and sisters. Soon the forest floor is covered with baby lizards. They all want to explore their new world.

Baby lizards are not raised by a mother or father lizard. Young lizards are born knowing what they have to do to survive in the rain forest.

Little Lizard is still small enough to fit in a human hand. She could grow up to be six feet long when she's older, though!

Little Lizard is dazzled by the many interesting sounds of the rain forest. She flicks her long tongue and bobs her head. In front of her, an army of ants carries leaves across the sandy floor of the forest.

Now Little Lizard is hungry for food. She leads a group of lizards across a trail of leaves. A movement catches her eye. Gulp! Little Lizard snaps up her first meal: a tasty termite. She eats a few more termites before moving on.

The lizards climb up a big tree near the river. The green leaves hide them well.

A dark shadow passes over the lizards' hiding spot on the mangrove tree. It is a hawk on the hunt. The hawk flies over the branch that Little Lizard is resting on.

She naturally knows just what she has to do. Her claws let go of the tree branch. Little Lizard is falling! She hits the water with a splash. 🐾

Little Lizard is a very good swimmer. She paddles toward a water lily and climbs on the leaf. Her long legs carry her from lily pad to lily pad. She reaches the shore and keeps on running.

Little Lizard hops over to a fallen tree trunk. All the other lizards are gone. Little Lizard seems to be alone now, but she is safe.

Little Lizard discovers she is not alone, and not at all safe. The tree trunk under her starts to roll! Little Lizard sees that the tree trunk was really a tapir, a forest animal that looks like a pig with a long snout. She leaps onto a nearby branch.

The tapir moves on to a better resting place. Little Lizard runs for the nearest tree. 🐾

Little Lizard is safe at last! But wait. She is not the only lizard in this tree. The other one is full-grown. He's four feet long! And he's not about to share his hideout.

The adult lizard swings his long tail. Clearly, the young lizard is not welcome in this tree! Little Lizard jumps out of the tree. 🐾

Little Lizard is back on the ground again. This is not where she wants to be! Iguanas like to be high in the trees, where they can warm themselves in the sun. Little Lizard looks up, searching for her special place. She looks right into the eyes of a jaguar! The jaguar growls loudly at her. Then Little Lizard is off and running again.

Little Lizard finally finds a safe place. This thick bush has plenty of delicious fruit for her to eat. It looks like Little Lizard will be just fine after all.